wasp

sun

Usborne Little Picture Dictionary

Illustrated by Christyan Fox

Designed by Keith Newell

bird

rain

castle

a

airport ....

apple ....

arm ....

Aa

armchair ....

aubergine ....

Bb

baby ....

B b

bag ....

baker's ....

ball ....

B b

banana ....

bank ....

bath ....

B b

bathroom ....

beach ....

bedroom ....

Bb

bee ....

bike ....

bird ....

B b

birthday ....

biscuits ....

boat ....

Bb

book

boots

bowl

B b

boy ....

bread ....

brush ....

Bb

bus ....

butcher's ....

butter..............................

C c

cake ....

camera ....

campsite ....

C c

candle ....

car ....

carrot ....

C c

cash machine ....

castle ....

cat ....

C c

chair ....

checkout ....

cheese ....

Cc

chemist's ....

chips ....

chocolate ....

C c

church ....

cloud ....

coat ....

C c

coffee ....

computer ....

countryside ....

C c

cow ....

cup ....

cupboard ....

Dd

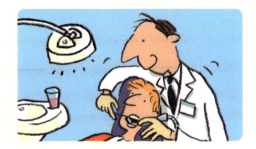

dentist ....

doctor ....

dog ....

Dd

door ....

dress ....

duck ....

Ee

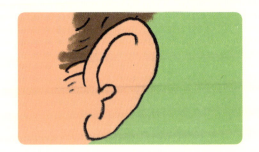

ear ....

egg ....

eyes ....

Ff

family ....

fireworks ....

fish ....

Ff

flat ....

flower ....

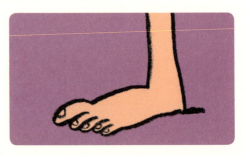

foot ....

F f

football ....

forest ....

fork ....

Ff

fruit ....

fruit juice ....

funfair ....

Gg

garden ....

girl ....

glass ....

G g

goat ....

grapes ....

green beans ....

Hh

hair ....

hand ....

hat ....

Hh

head ....

hen ....

holiday ....

Hh

hair ....

hand ....

hat ....

Hh

head ....

hen ....

holiday ....

Hh

horse

hospital

hotel

Hh

house ....

I i

ice cream ....

J j

jumper ....

Kk

key

kitchen

knife

L1

lake ....

lamp ....

leg ....

L1

lemon ....

living room ....

Mm

man ....

Mm

market ....

meat ....

milk ....

Mm

mobile phone ....

money ....

moon ....

Mm

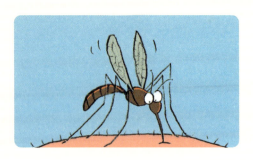

mosquito ....

mountain ....

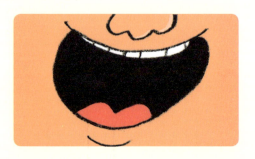

mouth ....

Nn

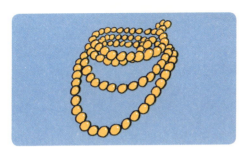

necklace ....

nose ....

Oo

onion ....

O o

orange ....

P p

pasta ....

peach ....

P p

pear ....

peas ....

pen ....

P p

pencil ....

pepper ....

petrol station ....

Pp

pineapple ....

plane ....

plant ....

Pp

plate ....

postcard ....

post office ....

Pp

potato ....

present ....

Rr

rain ....

Rr

restaurant ....

rice ....

river ....

Rr

road ....

rubbish bin ....

Ss

salad ....

S s

sales ....

sandals ....

scarf ....

S s

school ....

sea ....

shampoo ....

S s

sheep ....

shirt ....

shoes ....

S s

shops ....

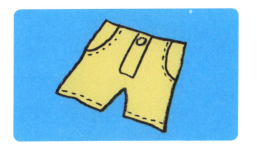

shorts ....

shower ....

S s

skirt ....

sky ....

snow ....

S s

soap ....

socks ....

sofa ....

S s

spoon ....

stadium ....

stamps ....

S s

star ....

street ....

suitcase ....

S s

sun ....

sun cream ....

sunglasses ....

S s

supermarket ....

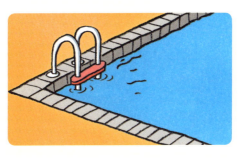

swimming pool ....

swimsuit ....

Tt

table ....

tea ....

teeth ....

Tt

television ....

tennis ....

toilets ....

Tt

tomato ....

toothpaste ....

tourist office ....

Tt

towel ....

town ....

train ....

Tt

train station ....

tree ....

trolley ....

Tt

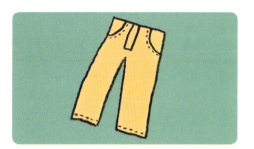

trousers ....

Vv

vegetables ....

Ww

washbasin ....

Ww

wasp ....

watch ....

water ....

Ww

wind ....

window ....

woman ....

Numbers

1
one ....

2
two ....

3
three ....

4
four ....

5
five ....

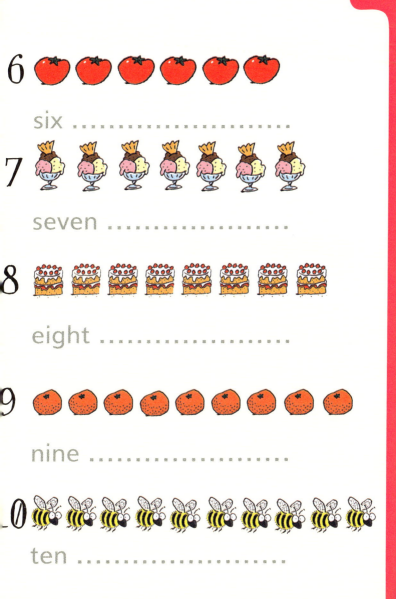

6 six ....

7 seven ....

8 eight ....

9 nine ....

10 ten ....

Colours

 red ....

 blue ....

 green ....

 yellow ....

 brown ....

 pink ....

 purple ....

 orange ....

 grey ....

 black ....

 white ....

Useful words

Seasons

spring ....

summer ....

autumn ....

winter ....

Days of the week

Monday ....

Tuesday ....

Wednesday ....

Thursday ....

Friday ....

Saturday ....

Sunday ....

Months of the year

January ....

February ....

March ....

April ....

May ....

June ....

July ....

August ....

September ....

October ....

November ....

December ....

Useful words

Shapes

square ....

circle ....

triangle ....

rectangle ....

octagon ....

Family words

father ....

mother ....

sister ....

brother ....

cousin ....